# BRYCE CANYON NATIONAL PARK

## A TRUE BOOK

by
**David Petersen**

**Children's Press®**
A Division of Grolier Publishing

New York  London  Hong Kong  Sydney
Danbury, Connecticut

For Sialia Baizel

*Reading Consultant*
**Linda Cornwell**
*Learning Resource Consultant*
*Indiana Department of*
*Education*

Some of the world's most oddly shaped rocks are found at Bryce Canyon National Park.

Library of Congress Cataloging-in-Publication Data

Petersen, David, 1946-
    Bryce Canyon National Park / by David Petersen.
        p.   cm. — (A true book)
    Includes index.
    Summary:  Describes the history, sights, and facilities of Bryce
Canyon National Park in Utah.
    ISBN 0-516-20048-8  (lib. bdg.)      ISBN 0-516-26094-4  (pbk.)
    1.  Bryce Canyon National Park  (Utah)—Juvenile literature.
[ 1.  Bryce Canyon National Park  (Utah)   2.  National parks and reserves.]
I.  Title.  II.  Series.
F832.B9P48   1996
979.2'52—dc20                                                              96-1183
                                                                                   CIP
                                                                                    AC

# Contents

# Bryce Canyon National Park

Bryce Canyon National Park covers 35,835 acres (14,500 hectares) in southern Utah. Bryce Canyon is an enchanted kingdom of rock formations. Its strangely-shaped and colored rocks look like castles, giant hammers, and sinking ships.

The rock people of Bryce Canyon

There are lots of rock "people" at Bryce, too.

The Southern Paiute people still tell a very old story about the stone people of Bryce Canyon.

Long ago, according to the Paiute, before the Europeans or even the American Indians, the Legend People lived at Bryce Canyon. The Legend People were actually animals, though they looked like people.

Paiute Indians settled the land near Bryce Canyon long before Europeans arrived there.

The Legend People had a god named Coyote. One day, they angered Coyote and, as punishment, Coyote used his magical powers to turn the Legend People to stone.

With a little imagination, you can still see the Legend People at Bryce. Some are sitting down. Others are standing or marching in rows. And all are still wearing the red, pink, purple, and yellow body paint they wore when Coyote turned them to stone.

According to Southern Paiute legend, the Legend People were turned to stone.

That is a fascinating story. But, studies by today's earth scientists, called geologists, provide evidence of how the stone cities and people of Bryce actually came to be.

# Hoodoo Science

The geologists say that about 60 million years ago, southern Utah was a low, flat area with many lakes and streams. For millions of years, the streams washed sediment—silt, sand, and clay—into the lakes. Eventually, the lakes filled with sediment and dried up. Over the centuries, the muddy sediment hardened into a soft rock called limestone.

About 13 million years ago, pressure inside the Earth began pushing up a great block of land. This huge land area included parts of what are now Utah, Arizona, Colorado, and New Mexico.

# Limestone

There are many kinds of sedimentary rock and they have a variety of uses. Limestone is a very common type of sedimentary rock, but others are shale, sandstone and coal. Limestone is used in building roads and in making cement. The chalk used in classrooms is made up mostly of limestone. Limestone is also used to make products such as fertilizer, paper, glass, and water filters.

The block of land rose higher and higher, until it was nearly 1 mile (1.6 kilometers) above sea level. Today, we call this gigantic raised area the Colorado Plateau.

The Colorado Plateau then divided into several smaller plateaus separated by wide valleys.

One of these plateaus is called the Paunsaugunt Plateau, from a Paiute word meaning "home of the

Bryce Canyon National Park lies
on the Paunsaugunt Plateau.

beaver." The rocky, eastern slope of the Paunsaugunt Plateau is called the Pink Cliffs.

Together, the Paunsaugunt Plateau and the Pink Cliffs form Bryce Canyon National Park. Nature carved the Legend People from the color- ful limestone of the Pink Cliffs.

But geologists call Bryce's strange rock figures "hoodoos." How were these hoodoos carved from the Pink Cliffs?

When it rains, water rushes down the steep slope of the

The Pink Cliffs

Pink Cliffs. Each time this happens, a little soft lime-stone is washed away.

Through this slow process, called erosion, running water has worn deep gullies in the

Fins are thin layers of rock left standing between eroded gullies.

Pink Cliffs. Between these eroded gullies, thin walls of rock are left standing. These thin walls are called fins.

But erosion at Bryce hasn't stopped at gullies and fins. It

has gone on to cut many of the fins into the lone-standing columns of rock, called hoodoos.

Hoodoos aren't the only inter-esting rock formations at Bryce. In some places, water erosion has worn holes completely

This hole, called a window, was caused by erosion.

Arches (left) can be found along Queen's Garden Trail. Natural Bridge viewpoint (right) can be seen from the park's main road.

through fins. Smaller holes are called windows. Larger holes are called arches. You can see one big arch at the Natural Bridge viewpoint, along the park road.

# People At Bryce Canyon

Paiute people came to the Paunsaugunt Plateau to hunt animals and gather wild plants. But the plateau is very cold in winter, so no American Indians lived there year round.

In the 1870s, white settlers began moving into the Paria Valley, below the Pink Cliffs.

# THE
# Southern Paiute

When the Southern Paiute first inhabited the area that is now Bryce Canyon, their land ranged from the Mojave Desert in California to the Colorado River in Arizona, and north to central Utah. The Paiute people hunted antelope, deer, rabbit, and mountain sheep. They also gathered berries, nuts, roots, and seeds. Some Southern Paiute planted beans, corn, and squash. Today, about 1,800 Southern Paiute live on reservations and work in agriculture, crafts, tourism, and industry.

Ebenezer
Bryce

One of these settlers—
Ebenezer Bryce—built the
first road up onto the
plateau, so people took to
calling the place after him.

By the early 1900s, uncontrolled logging and livestock

Uncontrolled logging caused serious damage to Bryce Canyon.

grazing had seriously damaged the land. If something wasn't done soon, the special beauty of Bryce Canyon would be lost forever.

Finally, in 1923, the Pink Cliffs and the Paunsaugunt

Plateau were given protection as a national monument.

Since then, Bryce Canyon has been carefully protected—for people like you, as well as for the many wild creatures that live there. In 1928, Bryce Canyon became a national park.

President Warren G. Harding (far left) visited Bryce Canyon after it became a national park.

# Life At Bryce Canyon

Visitors enter Bryce Canyon National Park near the town of Tropic, Utah. There, the elevation is 6,600 feet (2,012 meters). At the far end of the 18-mile-long (29-kilometers) park road, the elevation is 9,105 feet (2,775 meters)—a rise of 2,505 feet (764 meters).

Different plants and animals have adapted to each life zone.

Air gets cooler with altitude, and rain and snow increase. For this reason, traveling from the bottom of the park road to the top brings visitors through three different life zones.

A life zone is a climate—the combination of temperature, moisture, and sunlight—that supports certain kinds of life.

The lower part of the park lies in the Upper Sonoran life zone. Here we find desert plants such as cactus, sage, pinyon pines, and juniper trees. Lizards, snakes, and many birds are also well adapted to life in this hot, dry climate.

The Transition life zone extends from near the Bryce Canyon

Red-tailed hawks (top left), blue grouse (top right), and horned lizards (bottom), can all be found in the Upper Sonoran life zone.

Bryce Canyon Visitor's Center (left) and giant ponderosa pines (right) are found in the Transition life zone.

Visitor's Center to beyond the park's two campgrounds. This is a pleasant climate.

The Transition life zone supports giant ponderosa pines, grassy meadows, and lots of wildlife. Squirrels and chipmunks are com-

Squirrels (top left), chipmunks (bottom left), mule deer (top right), and prairie dogs (bottom right) are abundant at Bryce Canyon National Park.

mon in the campgrounds. In the meadows live prairie dogs and big-eared mule deer.

The high, windy tip of the plateau lies in the Canadian life zone. Hardy spruce, fir, and aspen trees thrive here. Big, black, crow-like birds called ravens love the cold winds at the plateau's rim.

Pine, spruce, and fir trees thrive in the park's Canadian life zone (left). Ravens (below) live at the top of the plateau.

Black bears (left) and bull elk (below) are the largest animals that live in Bryce Canyon National Park.

All together, Bryce Canyon supports more than 164 kinds of birds, 53 kinds of mammals, 11 kinds of reptiles, and 4 kinds of amphibians.

But the most amazing living things of all at Bryce Canyon are the bristlecone and limber pines. These trees cling to the highest, coldest, windiest points of the plateau.

By conserving energy through slow growth, limber and bristlecone pines have very long lives. One gnarly old bristlecone near Rainbow Point is more than 1,800 years old!

Limber pines (left) grow very slowly over many years. This bristlecone pine (right) at Rainbow Point is more than 1,800 years old.

# Exploring Bryce Canyon

As you can see, there are two exciting worlds to explore at Bryce Canyon National Park—the lush, green world atop the Paunsaugunt Plateau and the spooky hoodoos of the Pink Cliffs. You can get a taste of both of these worlds from the park's many roadside viewpoints. But to really

Visitors explore the Queen's Garden Trail.

experience Bryce, you will want to hike some of the park's 50 miles (80 km) of foot trails.

One of the most popular hikes down into the hoodoos

Hikers pick out some of Bryce Canyon's best-known hoodoos.

is the Queen's Garden Trail from Sunrise Point—the round-trip distance is just 1.4 miles (2.3 km). While you're down there, see if you can pick out the hoodoos named Queen's Castle, Queen Victoria, and Gulliver's Castle.

And why not name a few hoodoos yourself? There are plenty to go around. Use your imagination!

Up on the plateau, try the Bristlecone Loop Trail. The round trip is just one mile (1.6 km), starting from Rainbow Point.

The Bristlecone Loop Trail begins at Rainbow Point.

Bristlecone pines (left) are the oldest living residents of Bryce Canyon National Park. Park rangers lead visitors on tours of the park (above).

This easy trail follows the rim and offers spectacular views. It also provides a close-up look at Bryce's oldest residents—the bristlecone pines. Other attractions at Bryce include ranger-

Touring Bryce Canyon National Park by horse-back can be a fun and exciting adventure.

led nature walks, campfire pro-grams, geology talks, and even horseback rides!

Be sure to stop by the Visitor's Center before you leave. You'll find a wonderful

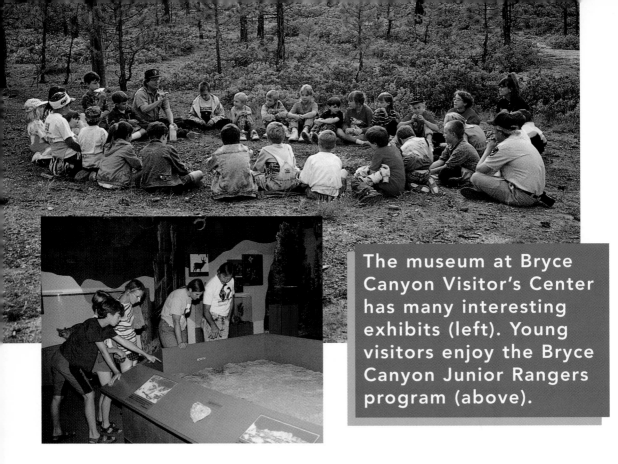

The museum at Bryce Canyon Visitor's Center has many interesting exhibits (left). Young visitors enjoy the Bryce Canyon Junior Rangers program (above).

museum there. And don't forget to ask about Bryce's special program for kids. It's called Junior Rangers. By taking part in this fun program, you can earn an official Bryce Canyon Junior Ranger patch!

There's so much to see and do at Bryce Canyon National Park. And no matter when you come, the Legend People will be there waiting very patiently for you.

The spectacular view of Bryce Canyon from Inspiration Point

# To Find Out More

Here are some additional resources to help you learn more about Bryce Canyon National Park.

 **Books**

 **Organizations**

Diamond, Lynell. **Let's Discover Bryce and Zion National Parks.** Mountaineers, 1990.

Fradin, Dennis. **Utah.** Children's Press, 1993.

Mead, Robin, et al. **Our National Parks.** Smithmark, 1993.

Weber, Michael. **Our National Parks.** Millbrook Press, 1994.

**Bryce Canyon National Park**
Bryce Canyon, UT 84717
801-834-5322

**National Park Service**
Office of Public Inquiries
P.O. Box 37127
Washington, DC 20013
202-208-4747

**Western Region**
National Park Service
600 Harrison Street
Suite 600
San Francisco, CA 94107

## National Parks and Conservation Association

1776 Massachusetts
  Avenue, NW
Washington, DC  20036
800-NAT-PARK
*natparks@aol.com*
*npca@npca.org*

## Great Outdoor Recreation Pages (GORP)

*http://www.gorp.com/gorp/
resource/US_National_Park/
main.htm*

Information on hiking, fishing, boating, climate, places to stay, plant life, wildlife, and more.

## National Park Foundation

CompuServe offers online maps, park products, special programs, a question-and-answer series, and in-depth information available by park name, state, region, or interest.  From the main menu, select *Travel,* then *Where To Go,* then *Complete Guide to America's National Parks.*

## National Park Service World Wide Web Server

*http://www.nps.gov*

Includes virtual tours, maps, essays.

## National Parks Magazine

*editorial@npca.org*

Focuses on the park system in general, as well as on individual sites.

**Note:**  Many of the national parks have their own home pages on the World Wide Web.  Do some exploring!

# Important Words

*fault* fracture line in the earth's crust

*geologist* person who studies the earth and its features

*gully* small valley

*joint* vertical fracture, or crack, in stone

*life zone* environment to which specific types of plants and animals have adapted

*sedimentary rock* rock, such as limestone and sandstone, formed by compressed layers of sand, silt, clay, or other sediment

# Index

# Meet the Author

David Petersen is a naturalist, writer, and teacher who lives in Durango, Colorado. He enjoys traveling and has visited each of the national parks about which he has written. Other titles by Mr. Petersen in the True Books series for Children's Press include: *Death Valley National Park*, *Denali National Park and Preserve*, and *Petrified Forest National Park*.